Overbeck s
Museum and Garden

Devon

THE NATIONAL TRUST

THE HOUSE

The house was built in 1913 as a comfortable Edwardian villa. Otto Overbeck retired here in 1928 and remained until 1937, when he left the house and garden to the National Trust, stipulating that it be renamed Overbeck's in his memory. The house is now a museum, which is as full of the unexpected as Overbeck himself. Here you can see a fascinating and diverse range of exhibits, with rooms devoted to natural history, local maritime history, children's toys and Overbeck's own family heirlooms – all of which we think will appeal to adults and children alike.

A COSMOPOLITAN COLLECTOR

Welcome to Overbeck's Museum and Garden. We hope this guide will help you to enjoy our extraordinary collection.

The place takes its name from Otto Overbeck. Although he was born in England, Otto Christopher Joseph Gerhardt Ludwig Overbeck was descended from a distinguished Dutch family. His parents were of mixed nationality: his father Dutch and Italian, his mother Prussian and French. Perhaps this cosmopolitan background accounted for his varied interests. A research chemist by profession, he was also an accomplished linguist, artist and inventor, and, as you will see, a keen collector.

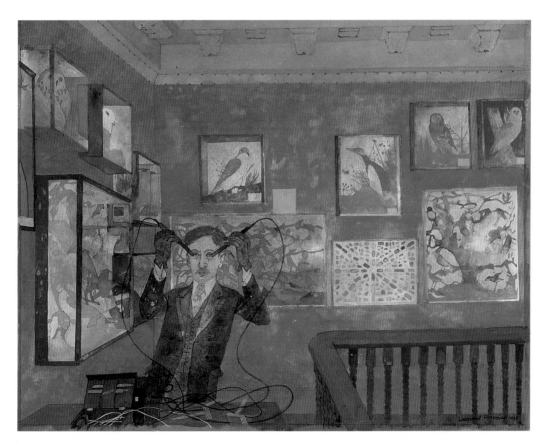

'Since completing my apparatus and using it on myself, I have practically renewed my youth.'
OTTO OVERBECK
ON HIS ELECTRICAL
REJUVENATOR, 1925

Opposite Otto Overbeck

Left Otto Overbeck demonstrating his electrical rejuvenator on himself; painted by Leonard Rosoman, 1990 (Foundation for Art)

TOUR OF THE HOUSE

THE STAIRCASE HALL

DID YOU KNOW?
The child's chair, often
thought to be a dunce's
chair, was based on a design
by the anatomist Sir Astley
Cooper (1768–1841). It was
specially designed to make
children sit up straight, to
avoid rounded shoulders.
This particular chair was
used in the dame school
at Salcombe.

Mechanical melodies

As you enter the museum, you will see that the handsome mahogany staircase is the central focus to the hall. You may also hear the music of the Polyphon. The story goes that Otto was in a bar and saw it playing. He was so fascinated that he asked the landlord if he would be prepared to swap it for a modern gramophone. The deal was done, and this extraordinary music box (dating from the 1890s) is now one of our most popular exhibits. Polyphons were built in Leipzig, but because of heavy import duty, the Manchester firm of Gouldman bought only the mechanical parts, which were then fitted into English-made cabinets.

A room within a room

Within this room is a reconstructed cottage parlour of the late 19th century. Here you can see a range manufactured by Lidstone's, a Kingsbridge foundry which supplied much of the metalwork for local houses and shipping. The two Windsor chairs were also made in the West Country, but the late 19th-century clock has come all the way from America. Standing on the carved elm chest is a harvest barrel used to carry beer or cider into the fields.

The wall cabinet contains a collection of Devon mottoware china.

Right Devon mottoware china

Far right The mantelpiece in the National Trust shop displays Doulton, Torquay and Elton ware

DID YOU KNOW?
The Polyphon works by
rotating metal discs with
projecting pins. These strike
a star-wheel, which in turn
plucks two metal combs,
with each tooth tuned to
a different note. You may
be surprised how clear the
notes sound. Why not help
us to compile our 'Top of
the Pops' chart from the
collection of around 50
discs? For a donation, we
will play your favourite tune
and record your choice.

Above The Polyphon

Left The Staircase Hall

DID YOU KNOW?
Overbeck's machines were all part of the 'Health and Vitality' movement that flourished at the '20s and '30s, producing a craze for cold baths, sleeping in the open air, and physical exercise.

Right Otto Overbeck's electrical rejuvenator

6

Otto Overbeck inventor

Take a look at the display of Otto Overbeck's inventions. A research chemist by profession, Overbeck was employed at a Grimsby brewery. Whilst there he developed a non-alcoholic beer, but it was never commercially produced, because the government insisted on levying a tax on it.

However, his most successful invention was the 'electrical rejuvenator' that he patented in the 1920s. He claimed that users could defy the ageing process by applying the electrodes from his device to their skin, and wrote in the *Daily Graphic* in 1925 that 'since completing my apparatus and using it on myself, I have practically renewed my youth'. He produced various pamphlets and books on his 'electrical theory of life', and successfully marketed the rejuvenator worldwide.

Pictures

You can judge for yourself Overbeck's youthful looks by his self-portrait on the wall and his artistic ability is evident in the beautiful pencil drawings and watercolours of boys and a fisher maid.

Among other pictures hanging in this room is a later version of a portrait dated 1560 of Cosimo de' Medici, the first Grand Duke of Tuscany (1519–74), from the studio of the Florentine painter Agnolo Bronzino. Overbeck's father probably acquired it while working at the Vatican in Rome.

The photographs on the walls and in the albums on the centre table are the work of local photographer Edward Chapman (1850–1939), taken around 1900. They form a fascinating collection of images from the past, showing unspoilt fishing villages on the south Devon coast, local characters and the landscape before the area became popular with tourists. You can see a collection of photographic equipment, including the Thornton Pickard camera used by Chapman in the Overbeck's Room.

Do you recognise the drawings of The Moult, Lord Devon's marine residence? Not far from Overbeck's, the house was built in 1764 and is one of Salcombe's earliest villas. The Moult has seen some important owners and visitors.

Left Cosimo de' Medici, Grand Duke of Tuscany, who ruled Florence in the mid-16th century and built the city's most famous art gallery, the Uffizi

Deadly devices

Look out for the display of gruesome traps used by gamekeepers on Lord Devon's estate. The spring gun was used to maim either poachers or smugglers, who often used the cliff paths. It was designed to shoot pellets or a bolt, which could cause crippling injuries. Equally lethal was the mantrap, which, although made illegal in 1827, was still in use at the end of the 19th century. The gin traps were designed to catch dogs, cats or rabbits.

Another unnerving collection shows handcuffs dating from the 18th and 19th centuries; the early ones are cruder, with flattened, heart-shaped keys.

The notorious John Lee from Babbacombe, known as 'The man they couldn't hang', wore one of these pairs of handcuffs. Lee was condemned to hang in 1884 for murdering his employer. However, the trap door failed to open three times, and his sentence was commuted to life imprisonment – a lucky escape!

Samplers

In complete contrast to the handcuffs, the early 19th-century samplers displayed on the walls were probably created by well-behaved children. Samplers were commonly worked as a form of education as well as art, and very often incorporated alphabets and numbers, followed by an uplifting psalm or verse, as in the two worked by Kezia Luckham. The map sampler probably dates from around 1800 and is interesting because of the old county titles and the unusual names used.

THE STAIRCASE AND LANDING

Natural history

In this part of the room you will see examples of Overbeck's natural history collection, which includes stuffed animals and birds, birds' eggs, fish, fossils, shells and insects. Assembled in the late 19th century, it represents a typical Victorian collection.

Right Handcuffs worn by the notorious John Lee of Babbacombe ('The man they couldn't hang') and a flintlock mantrap

Right and opposite Butterflies and stag beetles are displayed among the natural history collections on the Landing

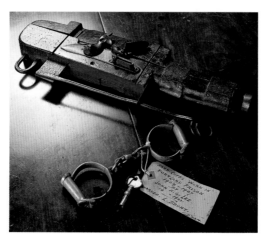

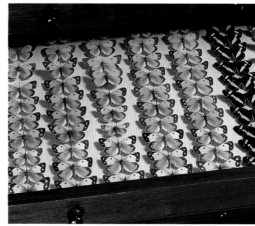

The Maritime Room celebrates Salcombe's past as a prosperous port. The scale models, paintings and photographs record ships that were built, sailed and lost in these waters.

A dangerous trade

The port of Salcombe was at its peak during the 1870s, when as many as 95 ocean-going vessels were using the haven. These ships plied a particularly arduous trade, leaving Salcombe for Cadiz, where they took on salt destined for Newfoundland. This cargo would then be exchanged for salt cod and shipped on to the Mediterranean, where it would be exchanged again for fruit before returning home. Many of these schooners were built here in Salcombe, and you can see examples of the tools used in the shipbuilding trade around the room.

Model ships

In this room we have several beautiful model ships on display. Ship models were often made by sailors to pass long hours in the doldrums; for example the ship's carpenter constructed the model of the *Eclipse*. Other models include a Brixham trawler, the *Onyx*, complete with net. Shipwrights produced wooden half-models to show a prospective client the lines of the vessel.

DID YOU KNOW?
One of the first schooners built in Salcombe was the *Phoenix*, a painting of which hangs in this room along with two portraits of her master, William Port. Built by Bonker in 1836, the *Phoenix* led an active trading life until 1842, when she set sail from Cardiff bound for Barcelona; neither ship nor crew were heard of again.

HMS *Captain* was an early example of a turret warship, powered by both sail and steam. The design of HMS *Captain* was the brainchild of a naval officer, Captain Cowper Coles. However, while still on its trials in April 1870, the ship capsized with the tragic loss of almost all the 500 crew.

Left The schooner *Phoenix* was built at Salcombe in 1836

Opposite A model of the Brixham trawler *Onyx*

For those in peril

The best-known wreck along this coastline is the *Herzogin Cecilie*, a Finnish barque loaded with wheat, which hit the Ham Stone near Soar Mill Cove. The story of the *Herzogin Cecilie* is told in the album on the ship's desk, and remains of her tensioning shackle and chain link are on display.

Pictures

Hanging on the wall is a picture of the *Restless*, a Salcombe trading vessel which was painted by one of the most prolific of British ship portraitists, Ruben Chappell (1870–1940). Unfortunately, a dredger ran her on the Thames in about 1913.

Furniture

The large oak desk in the centre of the room came from the counting house of the shipping agents G.C. Fox of Falmouth, where hand-written ledgers would record ship movements. On top of the desk are two brass tobacco machines patented by Rich of Bridgwater in the early 19th century. A coin would release the button to open the lid for the smoker to remove a plug of tobacco. The boxes were also known as honesty boxes, because it was possible to take more than your share from the machine.

On this desk you will also find albums and information sheets that tell further fascinating stories about the exhibits here.

Above The *Restless*

Right The *Mary Dare*

Left The wreck of the *Herzogin Cecilie* beached in Starehole Bay in 1936

SHELLS AND SCRIMSHAW

Shell-collecting was popular during the 18th and 19th centuries. Shells on display in the cabinet come mainly from the Americas and Australia. They would have been brought back by sailors who would also have painted the *ostrich eggs* and decorated the *sperm-whale teeth* (illustrated on the right), a folk art known as scrimshaw. Many of the other curios were collected by Mr Overbeck, including the armadillo handbag.

Above 19th-century dolls in the Overbeck's Room. These dolls were made from a variety of materials – wood, porcelain and even chocolate.

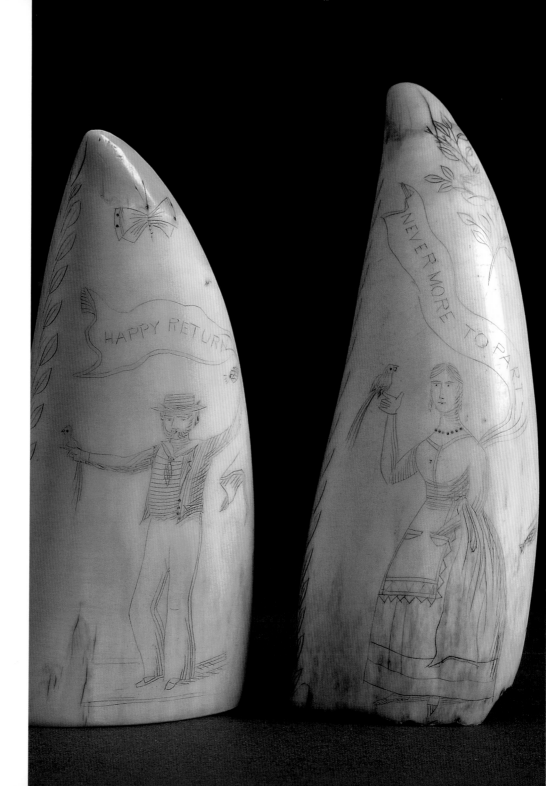

THE OVERBECK'S ROOM

Moving through to Overbeck's Room, you will see more of Otto's diverse collection of curios and family heirlooms.

Books

This room originally housed a library. Today it is still home to the three magnificent leather-bound volumes on Roman antiquities. These were written and illustrated by Otto Overbeck's ancestor, Bonaventura van Overbeke, in the late 17th century. The volumes were published in 1708 by Michael van Overbeke under the patronage of Queen Anne, whose insignia adorn the covers, when Michael was the Dutch Ambassador to England.

Dolls

In another cabinet you will find a collection of 19th-century dolls. Notice how dolls from this period often resembled adults rather than children: baby dolls did not become popular until the 1880s. Novelty dolls were also made, like the German example, with a revolving head to show one face sleeping, one crying and the last smiling.

The collection of dolls in national dress was made by Miss Irene Ellis and includes a pair of dolls resembling an elderly Chinese couple. Such dolls would probably have been given to children attending a missionary school.

THE SECRET ROOM

Hidden under the stairs, the Secret Room has been specially created by the National Trust for children and is full of toys. There are room settings from doll's houses, which belonged to the Overbeck family. Some of the other toys are imaginatively made from unusual materials, like the Bunt and Barpar Profiteers Shop, which is constructed out of sardine tins, and the provisions cupboard out of matchboxes.

Fred the ghost can often be found hiding in the Secret Room, where he loves to play among the toys.

DID YOU KNOW?
The rocking horse was given to Salcombe school in 1890. The best pupil of the week was allowed to ride the horse for fifteen minutes.

Below These grand volumes on the ancient monuments of Rome were written and illustrated by an ancestor of Otto Overbeck

THE GARDEN

The garden at Overbeck's was founded in 1901. Located just above the Salcombe Estuary, the favourable climate enjoyed on this southerly stretch of the coast has allowed an extraordinary garden to develop, protected from the worst of the weather by a shelter belt of surrounding woodland, while also enjoying some breathtaking sea views.

The first owner, Edric Hopkins, laid out much of the structure, creating a series of small enclosures and broad terraces, building the walls and castellations from the grey rock excavated and recovered from the cliff side. The Verekers bought the property in 1913, and being keen gardeners, continued to diversify the plantings. They were followed by Otto Overbeck in 1928, who believed he had found the perfect place to give free reign to his fascination with the exotic and sub-tropical.

Rare and tender plants were favoured from the beginning, and more than a hundred years later, some of these are still flourishing, notably a huge camphor tree, and some spectacular early-flowering magnolias. There is a strong Mediterranean influence at Overbeck's, suggested by the terraces, the gravel paths, the glazed pots, and by much of the planting. But the garden looks further afield for inspiration – to Africa, to the Far East, to South America – which is in keeping with the long tradition of growing an extending range of unusual plants here, which are not often found living outside in England.

It is an informal garden, with adventurous planting throughout. There are bold foliage contrasts, with luxuriant leaves set against the spikes of yuccas and agaves, complemented by rich swathes of hot colours in the long summer months. Wandering around the garden, it soon becomes clear that there are surprises around most corners.

From the flagpole in front of the house, where Otto Overbeck's coat of arms is usually flying, there is a wonderful view looking down the estuary towards Salcombe, one of the many maritime vistas that the garden offers. Turning to your right, take the rising path leading away from the house.

Follow this path until you come to a garden on a level, with four large flower beds.

Above The Conservatory

Right Otto Overbeck in his garden; painted by Leonard Rosoman

Above Agapanthus and gaura

Left The mild microclimate
of the garden allows exotics
like Chusan palms to flourish

Above Canna indica
'Purpurea' and crocosmias

Right Albert Joy's *First Flight*
in the Statue Garden

THE STATUE GARDEN

This garden takes its name from the bronze statue in the centre, *First Flight*, by Albert Bruce Joy (1842–1924). It was once the site of a tennis court, but by the 1920s the desire for more planting space meant that the flower beds had been cut into the grass. Now this area is dominated by lush plantings of tender perennials, including a good range of salvias, agapanthus and cannas, as well as kniphofias, inulas and heleniums. These are complemented by unusual annuals, wherever space allows. The Statue Garden is filled with colour and fragrance from early June through to the end of the autumn, and is a rich source of food for the many bees and butterflies that frequent Overbeck's.

The tall tree with glossy green leaves on the bank above the gravel path is a camphor, the largest of its type ever recorded in England. It is native to tropical Asia, and should suffer badly if the temperature were to drop below 10°C. However, it has thrived here for more than a hundred years, due to the extraordinary microclimate that also allows other tender plants to survive without winter protection.

Continue along the gravel path, heading through the stone pillars at the far end. This area is known as the **Secret Garden**, one of many hidden corners at Overbecks. By the end of the summer, the huge *Vitis coignetiae* vine adorning the railing has grown to make a trailing curtain. Moving past the tall date palm in the middle of the grass area, go towards the wall and look over.

Below, there are working greenhouses,

the gardeners' bothy with a terracotta-tiled roof in the Mediterranean style, and a parterre with clipped box hedging. This was planted in 1991 and established itself quickly. Orange and lemon trees stand out here in large glazed pots during the warmer months.

To the left of the parterre, there is a big swathe of banana palms. These plants have been grown here since the early 1920s, and several of the stems bear fruit each year. The small green bananas are not edible, but the flowers can be eaten.

Retrace your steps back through the Statue Garden, but this time, as you leave, take the path that leads upwards to your left. This takes you past a rare *Euonymus lucidus* tree on your right with leaves of red, yellow and green, and a view of the estuary framed by the branches. To the left, a vigorous *Wisteria macrobotrys* trained along the railings cascades dark blue flowers in the early summer.

Above The Statue Garden

Left The parterre

THE UPPER GARDENS

At the top of the path, there is a short flight of slate steps leading down to the *Gazebo Garden*. There is another sweeping view of the estuary from here, and a small sheltered seating area. The Riviera theme returns once more, with plantings of cistus, abelia and myrtle trees with cinnamon bark.

Going back up the steps and straight on takes you into the *Rock Dell*. The spiky plantings of phormiums, astelias, cordylines and fascicul019arias are softened by a profusion of argyranthemum daisies, combined with the succulent purple leaves of tall aeoniums.

The jagged rock face that is exposed here is a reminder that the garden has been created on a rugged cliff face. This is also one of the reasons it is possible to grow such a wide range of tender plants throughout the garden. The millions of minute rock particles from the cliff side mean that the soil is very free-draining, stopping the plants from rotting in excessively wet conditions, while also preventing winter frosts from penetrating .

Take the steps up to the *Picnic Area*, the highest point of the garden. A small olive grove is slowly being established here.

Right The view from the garden over Salcombe estuary

Above The Rock Dell

Left A glimpse of the Tropics in Devon

Right Chusan palms and tall spires of echiums

THE BANANA GARDEN

Walk back down, through the Rock Dell, taking the steep path to your right. There is a small raised rock circle to your left with a miniature cactus garden. Rather than return to the house, follow the path right around the curve until you come to a archway. Here you suddenly find yourself in a little jungle, surrounded by high stone walls and filled with ferns and lush green foliage.

This is the most sheltered part of the garden, and is home to some of the most tender tropical plants at Overbecks. These include specie fuchsias from South America, brugmansias, hedychiums, tree ferns and a good number of different types of bananas. Many of these were first introduced here in 2002, to continue to extend the range of plants in the garden.

The bananas are one of the few plants that need some added protection. Each winter, the stems are wrapped in fleece to keep some warmth in, and then covered with a green mesh overcoat to keep some of the rain out.

A large *Magnolia campbellii* presides over this area, an unforgettable sight in early spring, when it is laden with hundreds of deep pink flowers. This famous old tree was planted here in 1901, when the garden was first laid out, and despite tipping over in winter 1999 after heavy rain, it continues to show healthy growth.

Another significant tree nearby is the *Acacia pravissima*, against the wall by the archway, probably the largest of its kind in England, and smothered in fragrant yellow flowers each spring.

There is yet another small garden on the terrace below the bananas, reached via the stone steps. It is a tranquil corner, where citrus fruits are to be found in the summer, a good place to sit for a while as the scents of orange and lemon blossom drift all around.

Turn back and take the path out through the archway, heading down the long straight path. To your left, there is a gravelled bank filled with ornamental grasses, agaves and yuccas, as well as various restios from South Africa. The tall trees are Chusan palms, and are to be found throughout the garden, most dating back to the 1930s.

As you move along the path, to the right you will see that there are a series of narrow terraces, where exotic flowering shrubs are growing – banksias, proteas and metrosideros.

THE WOODLAND

Further on down the path, there is a row of Lantern Trees to your left, *Crinodendron hookerianum* from Chile.

Keep going along the path until you reach the shade. Overbeck's is no more than three hectares, but it is unusual and intricate, with many different hidden aspects and surprises. It even has its own small woodland. The older trees are mostly beech and evergreen oak, predating the house and garden, providing shelter from cold north winds.

As you leave, if you turn left, back up the drive, you can return to Overbeck's and enjoy the wonderful views once more.

Above The Banana Garden

EXPLORING THE SALCOMBE COAST

The National Trust cares for thirteen miles of coastline around the picturesque harbour of Salcombe and the Kingsbridge estuary. To the east lies Prawle Point, the southernmost point of Devon, which is an important landfall for migrating birds and so is a popular spot for birdwatchers. To the west, the rugged stretch of headlands and coves extends six miles to Hope Cove. This unspoilt area of south Devon has been designated one of Britain's heritage coasts. There is a network of coastal paths for walkers, and details of two suggested walks between Overbeck's and Bolt Head are given in a booklet available in the shop.

Opposite The view from Gammon Head towards Salcombe

The National Trust

is a registered charity

is independent of government

was founded in 1895 to preserve places of historic interest or natural beauty permanently for the benefit of the nation

relies on the generosity of its supporters, through membership subscriptions, gifts, legacies and the contribution of many thousands of volunteers

protects and opens to the public over 200 historic houses and gardens and 49 industrial monuments and mills

owns more than 244,000 hectares (603,000 acres) of the most beautiful countryside and 575 miles of outstanding coast for people to enjoy

If you would like to become a member or make a donation, please telephone 0870 458 4000 (minicom 0870 240 3207); write to: The National Trust, PO Box 39, Warrington WA5 7WD; or see our website at: www.nationaltrust.org.uk

Text by Hugh Meller, Vicki Pepper and Nick Stewart

Photographs: National Trust pp.2 (right), 13; NT/David Garner front cover, pp.4 (left and right), 5 (left and right), 6, 8 (right), 9, 10, 11, 12 (top left), 14 (left and right), 15, 18 (right); NT/Nick Stewart pp.21 (right), 23; National Trust Photographic Library p.7; NTPL/Mark Bolton pp.17 (right), 18 (left), 19 (bottom); NTPL/Derek Croucher pp.2 (left), 20, 21 (left), 22, 24; NTPL/John Gollop p.8 (left); NTPL/John Hammond p.12 (bottom right); NTPL/Nigel Hicks p.19 (top); NTPL/Nick Meers p.16 (top); NTPL/George Wright pp.1, back cover; Leonard Rosoman/Foundation for Art/NTPL pp.3, 16 (bottom).

© 2004 The National Trust
Registered charity no.205846
ISBN 1-84359-107-3

Designed by Rose-Innes Associates

Print managed by Centurion Press Ltd (HGP) for the National Trust (Enterprises) Ltd, 36 Queen Anne's Gate, London SW1H 9AS

Overbeck's Museum was created by Otto Overbeck, who filled
the house with his extraordinary collection of natural history,
toys, musical instruments and local maritime history. Thanks
to the mild microclimate, tender exotics flourish in his garden,
which enjoys superb views over the Salcombe estuary.

ISBN 1-84359-107-3

9 781843 591078 >

The Homewood

First floor

Front cover A view from the garden

Opposite The double-light wall-fittings in the Entrance Hall were designed by Patrick Gwynne about 1963 'for Witley Court. They appear in the view of the entrance hall illustrated on p.15

Back cover The landing and top of the spiral staircase